DINOSAURS RULED!

PLESIOSAURUS

LEIGH ROCKWOOD

PowerKiDS
press™
New York

Published in 2012 by The Rosen Publishing Group, Inc.
29 East 21st Street, New York, NY 10010

First Edition

Editor: Joanne Randolph
Book Design: Kate Laczynski

Photo Credits: Cover, title page by Brian Garvey; cover background (palm tree leaves) © www.iStockphoto. com/dra_schwartz; cover background (tree trunks) iStockphoto/Thinkstock; cover background (mountains, land, water), pp. 4–5, 6–7, 10 (top), 12, 13, 14–15, 17 (left, right), 18, 20–21 © 2011 Orpheus Books Ltd.; p. 8 © www.iStockphoto.com/Joe Pogliano; p. 9 D'Arco Editori/Getty Images; pp. 10–11 Harry Taylor/ Getty Images; p. 16 © www.iStockphoto.com/hsvrs; p. 19 © www.iStockphoto.com/Agnieszka Szymczak; p. 22 AFP/Getty Images.

Library of Congress Cataloging-in-Publication Data

Rockwood, Leigh.
 Plesiosaurus / by Leigh Rockwood. — 1st ed.
    p. cm. — (Dinosaurs ruled!)
 Includes index.
 ISBN 978-1-4488-4970-3 (library binding) — ISBN 978-1-4488-5090-7 (pbk.) —
 ISBN 978-1-4488-5091-4 (6-pack)
 1. Plesiosaurus—Juvenile literature. I. Title.
 QE862.P4R63 2012
 567.9'37—dc22

                                        2011000099

Manufactured in the United States of America

CPSIA Compliance Information: Batch #WS11PK: For Further Information contact Rosen Publishing, New York, New York at 1-800-237-9932

CONTENTS

MEET THE PLESIOSAURUS

If you thought the plesiosaurus was a **marine** dinosaur, you were wrong! The plesiosaurus was not a dinosaur. It was part of a group of marine **reptiles** with flippers called plesiosaurs. These ancient reptiles had long necks, small heads, and large bodies. The word "plesiosaurus" means "near lizard."

Plesiosaurus **fossils** help **paleontologists** learn about the animal. They use these clues to come

The plesiosaurus was also part of a group of marine reptiles called sauropterygians. "Sauropterygia" means "lizard flippers."

up with theories, or ideas, about what the animal's life was like. These theories can change as new discoveries are made. They can help us imagine the life of an animal that has been **extinct** for millions of years.

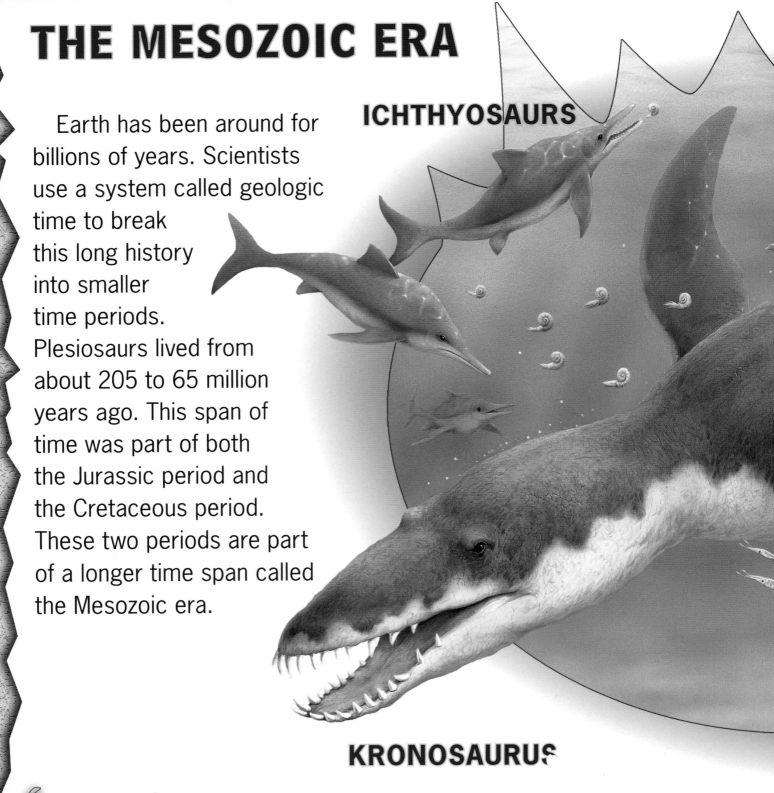

THE MESOZOIC ERA

ICHTHYOSAURS

Earth has been around for billions of years. Scientists use a system called geologic time to break this long history into smaller time periods. Plesiosaurs lived from about 205 to 65 million years ago. This span of time was part of both the Jurassic period and the Cretaceous period. These two periods are part of a longer time span called the Mesozoic era.

KRONOSAURUS

The plesiosaurus lived during the Late Jurassic period and became extinct 65 million years ago, at the end of the Cretaceous period. This is the same time that the dinosaurs became extinct. Paleontologists have many theories about why so many animals died out at once. Some ideas as to the cause include climate change or volcanic activity.

Plesiosaurs were not the only kind of marine reptile. Ichthyosaurs and pliosaurs, such as the giant kronosaurus, were other kinds of marine reptiles.

PLESIOSAUR

WHERE DID THE PLESIOSAURUS LIVE?

Earth looked very different during the Mesozoic era from the way it does today. During the Jurassic period, the **continents** as we know them were one large landmass called Pangaea. By the end of the Cretaceous period, this landmass had started to break apart. There were seas in the middle of Pangaea as well as around it. Plesiosaurs lived in seas all around

This fossilized fish was found in Wyoming. Prehistoric oceans once covered Wyoming. Over time, though, the land was pushed above the surface.

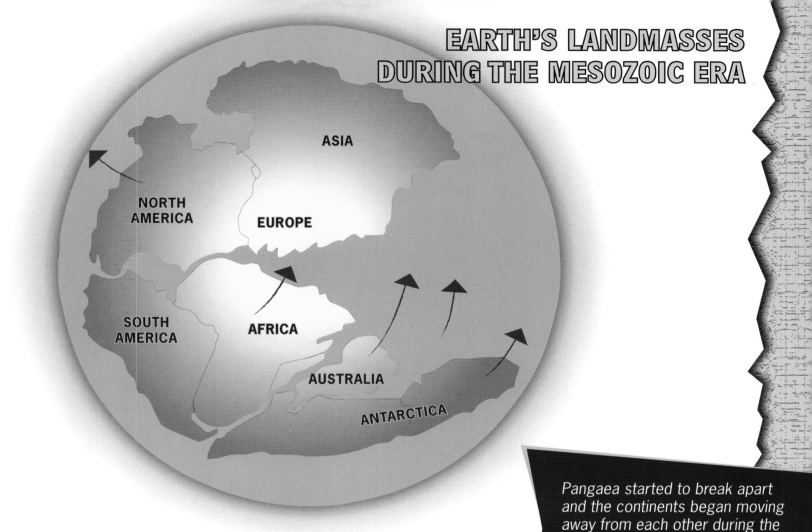

ASIA

NORTH AMERICA

EUROPE

SOUTH AMERICA

AFRICA

AUSTRALIA

ANTARCTICA

Pangaea started to break apart and the continents began moving away from each other during the time plesiosaurs swam in Earth's oceans. The continents continue to move today.

the world. Plesiosaurus fossils have been found in England and Germany.

Fossils form in **sedimentary rocks**. Sediment is made up of rocks, mud, and sand. When layers of sediment are pressed together over millions of years, they form rocks. Fossils form when layers of sediment cover dead plants or animals.

THE PLESIOSAURUS'S BODY

DINO BITE

Even though it is not possible, some people think the mythical Loch Ness monster is a plesiosaurus!

A full-grown plesiosaurus was about 15 feet (5 m) long and weighed about 1,000 pounds (454 kg). It had a small head, a long neck, and a streamlined body with four flipperlike limbs. As a **predator**, it needed to hunt and eat a lot of animals to feed its large body.

Even though the plesiosaurus lived in the water, it is important to remember that it was not a fish but a reptile. This means that it needed to come up to the surface to breathe air. This has led paleontologists to theorize that the plesiosaurus had an earlier relative that lived on land.

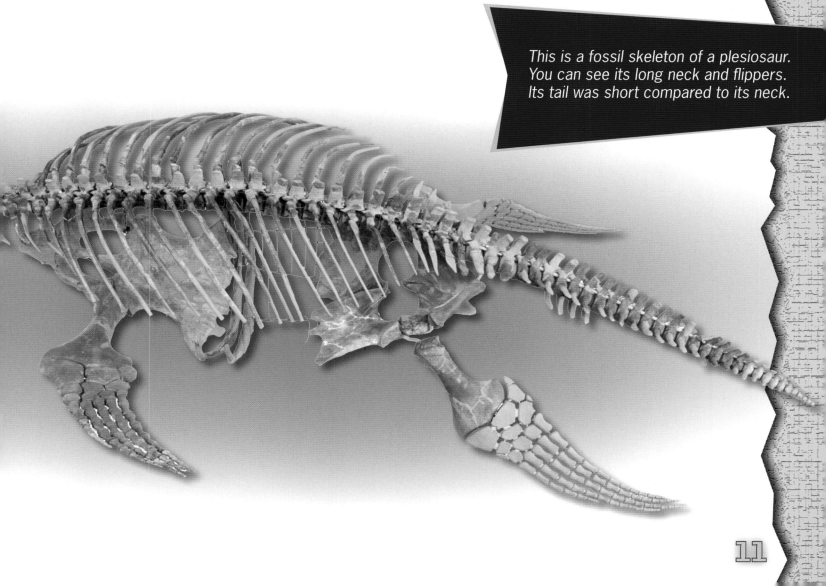

This is a fossil skeleton of a plesiosaur. You can see its long neck and flippers. Its tail was short compared to its neck.

LONG NECKS

As did other plesiosaurs, the plesiosaurus had a long neck. Paleontologists believe that its long neck helped it catch prey swimming in the sea. Although the plesiosaurus used to be shown with its neck bent

The plesiosaurus had a long neck that it could bend from side to side. It could also bend it up to go to the top of the water to breathe.

The elasmosaurus was a plesiosaur known for its extra long neck. Its neck was more than 20 feet (6 m) long and it had 70 vertebrae, or neck bones.

into tight curves, today's paleontologists believe its neck was less flexible than that.

Later plesiosaurs had even longer necks than the plesiosaurus. In some **species**, the length of its neck made up half of the animal's total body length!

SINK OR SWIM

DINO BITE

Just as did some dinosaurs, modern crocodiles, alligators, and many birds swallow stones to help them break down food.

The plesiosaurus swam underwater using its four flipperlike limbs. You might think that having four flippers would have made the plesiosaurus a fast swimmer. Paleontologists do not think this was the case, though. What was the advantage then of having four flippers? Plesiosaurs could make sudden starts and stops while swimming.

Plesiosaur fossils have been found with small stones in their stomachs.

The plesiosaurus's flippers had bones like those in a person's hand but many more of them. They swam by moving their front flippers up and the back ones down and then switching.

These small stones are **gastroliths**. Paleontologists once thought the job of the gastroliths was to help the animals sink down in the water to hunt. Today scientists think gastroliths mainly helped plesiosaurs break down food.

FEASTING ON THE SEA

The plesiosaurus was a **carnivore**, or a meat-eating animal. It ate different kinds of fish and shellfish living in its habitat.

One way that paleontologists have learned about the diets of plesiosaurs is by studying fossilized bits of

This is a fossil of a belemnite, which was one of the main foods the plesiosaurus ate.

The plesiosaurus ate shellfish called ammonites, like the ones shown here. The plesiosaurus had sharp teeth and powerful jaws.

digested food! It sounds gross, but this is a good way to know for sure what an animal ate. Scientists were surprised to find that plesiosaurs ate shellfish. After scientists studied the fossilized digested food, they changed their theory about the role of gastroliths. It is now clear that they helped break down shells.

LIFE AT SEA

Plesiosauruses swam in the open seas. They breathed air, as do today's dolphins and whales. That means that they needed to come to the top of the water to take a breath before diving under the water.

Plesiosaurs swam to the top of the water to breathe. They could then dive back underwater to hunt for food.

Green sea turtles have four flippers, just as plesiosaurs did. It is hard work for them to move on the beach when they lay their eggs. Some scientists think plesiosauruses would have made trips like this one to lay their eggs.

Paleontologists have not found enough fossil clues to know for sure if the plesiosaurus spent any time on land. Some scientists think the plesiosaurus came on land to lay eggs, as do today's sea turtles. Other scientists think it gave birth to live young in the water, as today's dolphins and whales do. No one knows for sure.

A WARM-BLOODED REPTILE?

Paleontologists have come up with a theory that the ancient marine reptiles, like the plesiosaurus, were **warm-blooded**, as are dolphins and whales. It had always been thought that ancient reptiles were cold-blooded, like today's reptiles.

Paleontologists came up with this theory after looking at the makeup of marine reptiles' teeth. There are slight differences in the makeup of the teeth of warm-blooded and

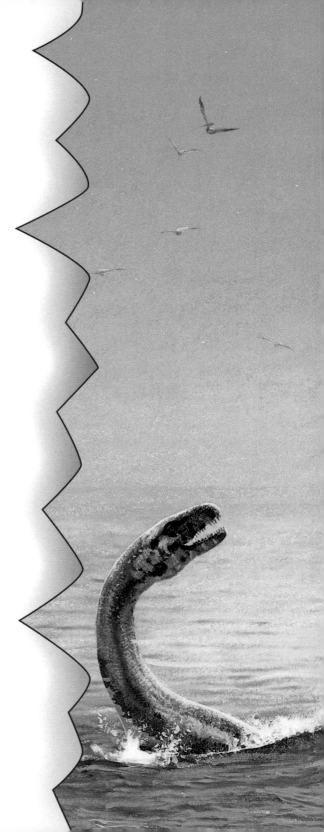

Fossilized teeth tell paleontologists a lot about an animal. Plesiosaurs had sharp, cone-shaped teeth and a jaw that could open very wide. These teeth were made for catching fish and other sea animals.

cold-blooded animals. The teeth of ancient marine animals, like the plesiosaurus, suggest they were warm-blooded. Being warm-blooded would have helped the plesiosaurus live better in cold water than cold-blooded animals could.

NO BONES ABOUT IT

A fossil hunter named Mary Anning found the first plesiosaurus fossil in 1821. She was one of the earliest fossil hunters. Her discoveries helped the paleontology field a great deal. They supplied a base of knowledge about these ancient animals.

Here a paleontologist unearths one of the many marine reptile fossils that have been found on islands in the far north of Norway, in the Arctic.

When paleontologists find a fossil, they carefully remove the rocks and dirt around it. They may leave the fossil attached to a larger rock until they can get it back to their lab to study. Many things about the plesiosaurus remain a mystery. However, every new fossil that is found adds something to what we know about this prehistoric marine reptile.

GLOSSARY

carnivore (KAHR-neh-vor) An animal that eats other animals.

continents (KON-tuh-nents) Earth's large landmasses.

extinct (ik-STINGKT) No longer existing.

fossils (FO-sulz) The hardened remains of dead animals or plants.

gastroliths (GAS-truh-liths) Stones swallowed by some animals to aid in the breakdown of food.

marine (muh-REEN) Having to do with the sea.

paleontologists (pay-lee-on-TO-luh-jists) People who study things that lived in the past.

predator (PREH-duh-ter) An animal that kills other animals for food.

reptiles (REP-tylz) Animals that are generally cold-blooded and that have thin, dry pieces of skin called scales.

sedimentary rocks (seh-deh-MEN-teh-ree ROKS) Stones, sand, or mud that has been pressed together to form rocks.

species (SPEE-sheez) One kind of living thing. All people are one species.

warm-blooded (WORM-bluh-did) Having a body heat that stays the same, no matter how warm or cold the surroundings are.

INDEX

WEB SITES

Due to the changing nature of Internet links, PowerKids Press has developed an online list of Web sites related to the subject of this book. This site is updated regularly. Please use this link to access the list:
www.powerkidslinks.com/dinr/plesi/